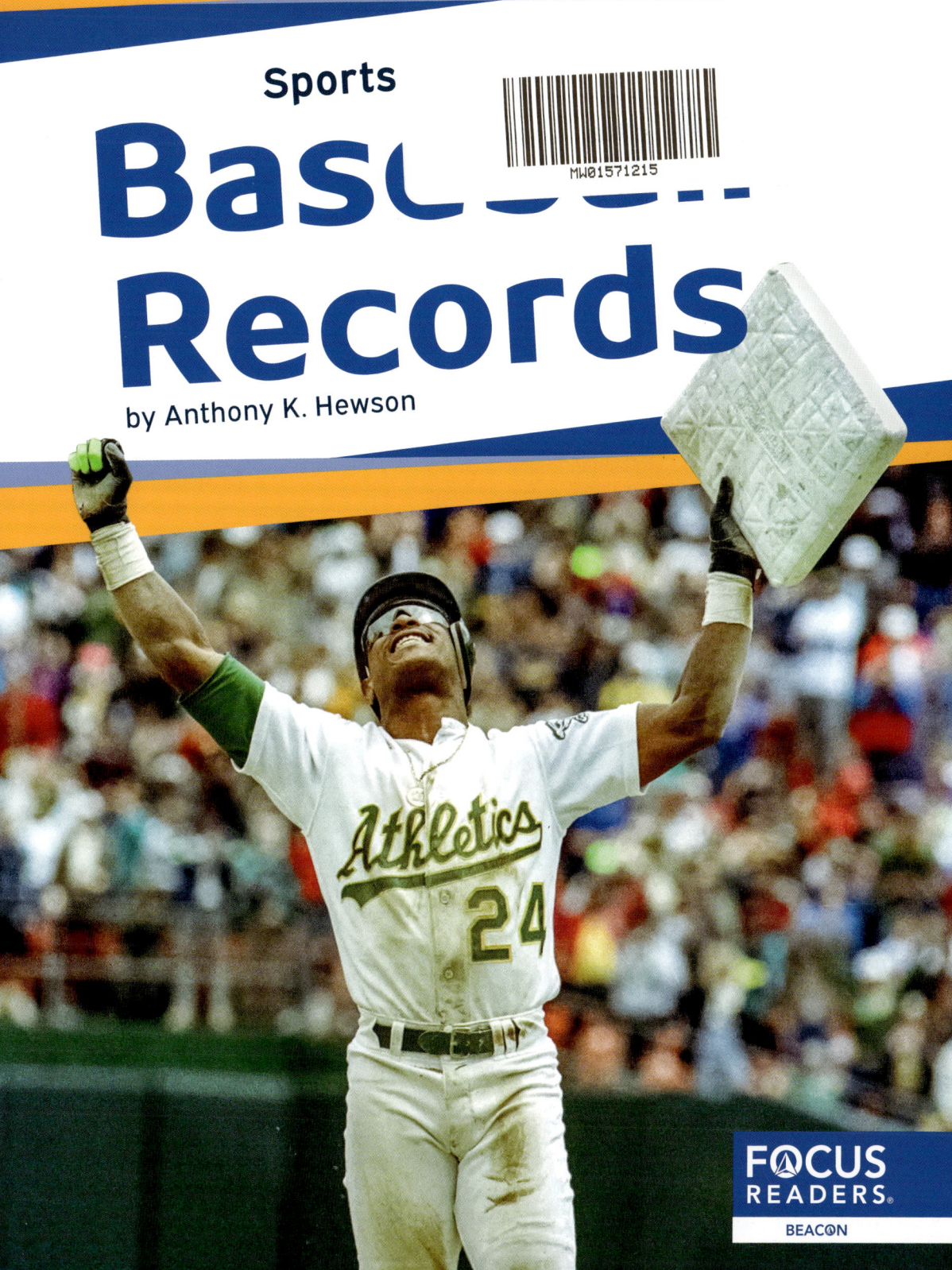

Sports

Baseball Records

by Anthony K. Hewson

www.focusreaders.com

Copyright © 2021 by Focus Readers®, Lake Elmo, MN 55042. All rights reserved. No part of this book may be reproduced or utilized in any form or by any means without written permission from the publisher.

Focus Readers is distributed by North Star Editions:
sales@northstareditions.com | 888-417-0195

Produced for Focus Readers by Red Line Editorial.

Photographs ©: Eric Risberg/AP Images, cover, 1, 13; Shutterstock Images, 4, 11, 29; Lenny Ignelzi/AP Images, 6; AP Images, 8, 21, 22, 27; Ted Mathias/AP Images, 14–15; Ian Johnson/Icon Sportswire/AP Images, 16; John Froschauer/AP Images, 18; Tony Gutierrez/AP Images, 25

Library of Congress Cataloging-in-Publication Data
Names: Hewson, Anthony K., author.
Title: Baseball records / by Anthony K. Hewson.
Description: Lake Elmo, MN : Focus Readers, 2021. | Series: Sports records | Includes index. | Audience: Grades 4-6
Identifiers: LCCN 2019060164 (print) | LCCN 2019060165 (ebook) | ISBN 9781644933596 (hardcover) | ISBN 9781644934357 (paperback) | ISBN 9781644935873 (pdf) | ISBN 9781644935118 (ebook)
Subjects: LCSH: Baseball--Records--United States--Juvenile literature.
Classification: LCC GV877 .H56 2021 (print) | LCC GV877 (ebook) | DDC 796.357021--dc23
LC record available at https://lccn.loc.gov/2019060164
LC ebook record available at https://lccn.loc.gov/2019060165

Printed in the United States of America
Mankato, MN
082020

About the Author

Anthony K. Hewson is a freelance writer, originally from San Diego, now living in the Bay Area with his wife and their two dogs.

Table of Contents

CHAPTER 1
Home Run King 5

CHAPTER 2
Incredible Careers 9

IMPOSSIBLE TO BREAK?
The Iron Man 14

CHAPTER 3
Tremendous Teams 17

CHAPTER 4
Super Seasons 23

Focus on Baseball Records • 28
Glossary • 30
To Learn More • 31
Index • 32

Chapter 1

Home Run King

Barry Bonds stepped into the **batter's box**. A packed stadium of San Francisco Giants fans cheered. The pitcher threw a fastball. Bonds crushed it 440 feet. It was his 71st home run of the 2001 season.

 Barry Bonds hit 586 home runs during his 15 seasons with the San Francisco Giants.

 Bonds won the Silver Slugger Award 12 times. This award goes to the league's best batters.

Fireworks soared into the sky.

Bonds was the new single-season home run king.

Bonds wasn't done. He hit two more homers that season to make the record 73. Six years later, Bonds broke the career home run record. He finished with a total of 762.

Home runs are special to baseball fans. Only three players have hit 700 or more. But home runs are not the only baseball records.

Fun Fact

In 2003, Bonds's 73rd home run ball sold to a collector for $450,000.

Chapter 2

Incredible Careers

Cy Young played from 1890 to 1911. Baseball was quite different in those days. But fans still talk about Young's dominance on the mound. He had 16 seasons where he won at least 20 games.

 Cy Young was elected to the National Baseball Hall of Fame in 1937.

Young racked up 511 wins during his career. That's nearly 100 more wins than the next-best pitcher.

The Closer

Mariano Rivera was famous for one pitch. It was the cut fastball. Batters knew it was coming. But they still couldn't hit it. Rivera was the **closer** for the New York Yankees. His job

The annual award for best pitcher in each league is named after Cy Young.

 Mariano Rivera pitched for 19 seasons in the major leagues.

was to come in at the end of the game and finish off a win. He had 652 **saves** in his career. That's the most saves in history.

Hit King

Pete Rose always played hard. That's how he earned the nickname "Charlie **Hustle**." Rose was also an amazing hitter. In 1985, Rose racked up the 4,192nd hit of his career. That broke the record held by Ty Cobb. Rose finished his career with 4,256 hits.

Man of Steal

Superman is known as the "Man of Steel." Rickey Henderson was the "Man of Steal." Henderson was the

Rickey Henderson set the all-time stolen base record in 1991.

greatest base stealer ever. He was fast, of course. But he also studied the game. He knew just the right time to steal. Henderson played from 1979 to 2003. In that time, he stole 1,406 bases.

IMPOSSIBLE TO BREAK?

The Iron Man

The Baltimore Orioles played a **doubleheader** on May 29, 1982. Cal Ripken Jr. played in the first game but not the second. It was the last game he missed for 16 years. Ripken holds the record for most games played in a row. Lou Gehrig had the old record of 2,130. But Ripken kept on going.

On September 28, 1998, Ripken took himself out of the lineup. His **streak** ended at 2,632 games. Nobody since has even come close. It's unlikely that Ripken's record will ever be topped.

Cal Ripken Jr. hits a triple in a 1995 game.

Chapter 3

Tremendous Teams

Two teams can claim to be the best regular-season team in history. The 1906 Chicago Cubs and 2001 Seattle Mariners each won 116 games. But the Cubs' record was slightly better.

 **The Chicago Cubs won the World Series in 1908. It took them 108 years to win the World Series again.**

 Bret Boone was a standout second baseman for the 2001 Seattle Mariners.

The Cubs played fewer games. As a result, they had 10 fewer losses. But neither team could win it all. The 1906 Cubs lost in the World Series.

The 2001 Mariners lost before even getting there.

Giant Hits

In 1930, the New York Giants were baseball's best hitting team. They set the record for **batting average** that year. They hit .319 as a team.

The 1927 Yankees were one of the greatest teams ever. They led the league in batting average, runs scored, and fewest runs allowed. They also won the World Series.

All but two starters hit .300. One player, Bill Terry, hit .401.

Amazing Pitching

It was good to be a pitcher in 1968. Pitching was dominant throughout baseball. Nobody was better than the St. Louis Cardinals. The Cardinals gave up only 472 runs.

Going into 2020, the San Francisco Giants had the most wins in baseball history. In 2018, they had become the first team to record 11,000 wins.

  Bob Gibson led the St. Louis Cardinals to the 1968 World Series.

That was the fewest ever. It helped that they had two future Hall of Famers. Bob Gibson and Steve Carlton both pitched for St. Louis that season.

Chapter 4

Super Seasons

Napoleon "Nap" Lajoie did it all in 1901. He led the American League in batting average, home runs, and runs batted in. Lajoie holds the record for highest batting average. In 1902, he hit an incredible .426.

 Nap Lajoie won five batting titles during his time playing in the major leagues.

Through 2019, only 28 batters had ever hit .400 or above. And it hadn't been done since 1941.

Hitting Machine

Ichiro Suzuki played in Japan during the early part of his career. He came to the United States in 2001. He was a 27-year-old **rookie**.

During his time in Japan and the United States, Ichiro Suzuki had 4,367 career hits. That is the most ever in pro baseball.

 Ichiro Suzuki had 10 seasons in a row with more than 200 hits.

He was also a hitting machine. In 2004, he set a record with 262 hits. Suzuki batted left-handed, and he had a quick swing. By the time he made contact with the ball, he was already stepping toward first base.

Bringing the Heat

Most pitchers dream of throwing a no-hitter. That means none of the opposing batters get a hit during the entire game. Nolan Ryan didn't just throw one no-hitter. He threw seven in his career. No other pitcher has come close to that record.

Fun Fact

Nolan Ryan also holds the record for career strikeouts with 5,714. Randy Johnson is in second place with 4,875 strikeouts.

 Nolan Ryan played for 27 seasons. He retired in 1993.

Records are part of baseball history. They help connect the past and present. Fans can look back and experience great players through their records. And records give today's players something to beat.

FOCUS ON
Baseball Records

Write your answers on a separate piece of paper.

1. Write a letter to a friend describing what you learned about baseball's biggest records.

2. Which baseball record do you think is the most impressive? Why?

3. Who holds the record for most home runs in a season?
- **A.** Pete Rose
- **B.** Barry Bonds
- **C.** Cal Ripken Jr.

4. What is the most likely reason that Ichiro Suzuki moved to the United States to play baseball?
- **A.** The United States has the best baseball league.
- **B.** The Japanese league was too difficult.
- **C.** He thought baseball would be easier in the United States.

5. What does **dominance** mean in this book?

*But fans still talk about Young's **dominance** on the mound. He had 16 seasons where he won at least 20 games.*

    A. the ability to stay healthy
    B. the ability to win often
    C. the ability to remember

6. What does **machine** mean in this book?

*He was also a hitting **machine**. In 2004, he set a record with 262 hits.*

    A. a person who is great at a task
    B. a piece of equipment
    C. a robot

Answer key on page 32.

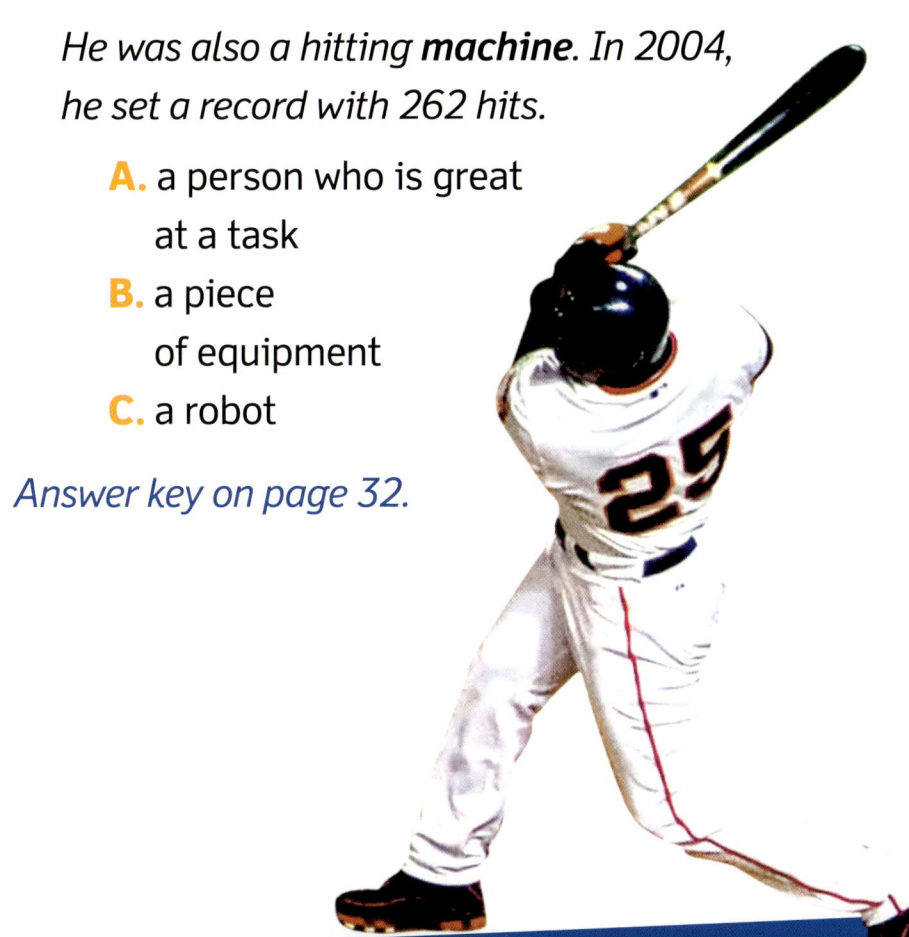

Glossary

batter's box
The outlined area near home plate where hitters have to stand when batting.

batting average
The number of hits a player has divided by the number of times at bat.

closer
A pitcher who usually pitches only the ninth inning to protect a lead.

doubleheader
Two games played back-to-back in a single day.

hustle
To give extra effort and speediness to any task.

rookie
A professional athlete in his or her first year.

saves
Statistics awarded when a pitcher protects a lead and gets the final outs of the game.

streak
When something happens many times in a row.

To Learn More

BOOKS

Abdo, Kenny. *History of Baseball*. Minneapolis: Abdo Zoom, 2019.

Fishman, Jon M. *Baseball's G.O.A.T.: Babe Ruth, Mike Trout, and More*. Minneapolis: Lerner Publications, 2019.

Monson, James. *Behind the Scenes Baseball*. Minneapolis: Lerner Publications, 2019.

NOTE TO EDUCATORS

Visit **www.focusreaders.com** to find lesson plans, activities, links, and other resources related to this title.

Index

B
Baltimore Orioles, 14
batting average, 19, 23
Bonds, Barry, 5–7

C
Chicago Cubs, 17–18
Cobb, Ty, 12

F
fastball, 5, 10

H
Henderson, Rickey, 12–13

L
Lajoie, Napoleon, 23

N
New York Giants, 19
New York Yankees, 10, 19

R
Ripken, Cal, Jr., 14
Rivera, Mariano, 10–11
rookie, 24
Rose, Pete, 12
Ryan, Nolan, 26

S
San Francisco Giants, 5, 20
Seattle Mariners, 17–19
St. Louis Cardinals, 20–21
Suzuki, Ichiro, 24–25

W
World Series, 18–19

Y
Young, Cy, 9–10

Answer Key: 1. Answers will vary; 2. Answers will vary; 3. B; 4. A; 5. B; 6. A